Your 40-Day Spiritual Alignment
A Journey Through Spiritual Mind Treatments

Dr. Nathalie Turgeon Ph.D.

All rights reserved. This book may not be reproduced in whole or in part, stored in a retrieval system, or transmitted in any form or by any means electronic, mechanical, or other without written permission of the author, except by reviewer, who may quote brief passages with source information in a review.

Cover and interior design: Nathalie Turgeon
ISBN paperback: 978-1-0695749-0-9
ISBN eBook: 978-1-0695749-1-6

Table of content

Note from the author 5
Why Spiritual Mind Treatment? 7
A Journey of Transformation 11
Why I Wrote This Book 13
First, what is a *Spiritual Mind Treatment*? 15
Day 1: Awakening to Truth 19
Day 2: Embracing Divine Love 20
Day 3: Releasing Fear 21
Day 3: Releasing Fear and Embracing Peace 23
Day 4: Cultivating Inner Peace 24
Day 5: Trusting the Divine Process 25
Day 6: Remembering Your Worthiness 26
Day 7: Stepping into Gratitude 27
Day 8: Aligning with Abundance 29
Day 9: Honoring Your Intuition 31
Day 10: Healing Old Wounds 33
Day 11: Expanding Consciousness 35
Day 12: Seeing with Spiritual Vision 37
Day 13: Letting Go of Control 39
Day 14: Welcoming Miracles 41
Day 15: Strengthening Inner Resilience 43
Day 16: Forgiving Yourself and Others 45
Day 17: Anchoring in Present Moment Awareness 47
Day 18: Embodying Self-Love 49
Day 19: Radiating Compassion 51
Day 20: Affirming Divine Order 53

Day 21: Embracing Change 55
Day 22: Releasing Limiting Stories 57
Day 23: Calling in Joy 59
Day 24: Deepening Faith 61
Day 25: Uncovering Inner Wisdom 63
Day 26: Aligning with Your Purpose 65
Day 27: Claiming Your True Power 67
Day 28: Trusting Divine Timing 69
Day 29: Cultivating Boundless Creativity 71
Day 30: Dissolving Doubt 73
Day 31: Living in Reverence 75
Day 32: Remembering Unity Consciousness 77
Day 33: Blessing Your Relationships 79
Day 34: Releasing Judgment 81
Day 35: Honoring Your Body as Sacred 83
Day 36: Inviting Playfulness and Lightheartedness 85
Day 37: Recognizing Divine Synchronicities 87
Day 38: Deepening Your Surrender 89
Day 39: Walking as Love 91
Day 40: Anchoring into Your Divine Identity 93
Conclusion: A Journey that Continues 97
About the Author 109

Note from the author

There is a moment in everyone's journey when the call to return inward becomes unmistakable. The world grows loud, the logical mind busy, and the heart whispers—softly at first, then more insistently, and peace and clarity reside not outside, but within.

Your 40-Day Spiritual Alignment: A Journey Through Spiritual Mind Treatments was born from that inner whisper as a tool for those ready to move beyond external solutions and into the sanctuary of Higher Truth. Spiritual Mind Treatment, as developed through metaphysical practice, is not about asking a distant power for favors or to save us; it is the art of aligning our conscious thought with Divine Intelligence. It is claiming, affirming, and embodying the Truth that already lives within us.

Each day in this 40-day journey offers a focused Spiritual Mind Treatment—a sacred dialogue with the Universe, centered on a theme relevant to real-life transformation. As within so without. Whether you are healing old wounds, aligning with your purpose, calling in True abundance alignment, or simply cultivating peace, this book is your sacred companion.

I invite you to read each Spiritual Mind Treatment aloud, breathe with it, pause with it. Let it speak *through* you, not just to you. Don't rush. Let yourself Be. Add what feels right to each as you let your Higher Self speak through your own voice. Let it awaken your remembrance of who you really are.

You are not broken. You are not lost. You are ready. You always were… your ego was just veiling it.

Let us begin.

Why Spiritual Mind Treatment?

An Inner Call to Remember

Throughout human history, people have prayed. In every tradition, in every corner of the world, the heart has reached towards something Greater—seeking comfort, healing, guidance, peace. But over time, for many, prayer became associated with pleading or asking from a place of lack, as if the Divine were distant, or conditional in Its love.

I don't know you but when we ask from a place of lack, it means that I believe I don't already have what I am wishing for. That was the one awareness that changed my way of praying and conversing with God, Divine Mind, Source, I AM, Divine Intelligence, no matter the name that feels right for you.

Spiritual Mind Treatment invites a different way of praying. It is not about begging for change but about *aligning* with what already *is*. It's a method of affirmative prayer that reminds us: we are not separate from the Source of Love, Wisdom, and Power. We are already part of it.

Rather than approaching the Divine from a place of disconnection, Spiritual Mind Treatment speaks directly from unity. It affirms what is True beyond appearances, beyond illusion. It is grounded in spiritual principles rather than religious dogma, making it accessible to anyone seeking to deepen their connection to the Higher Self, to the Sacred, to the Eternal.

While for many, this way of praying found voice in the New Thought movement through teachers like Ernest Holmes and others who recognized that consciousness creates experience, and that the mind aligned with Truth can bring profound transformation, it has been this way that Jesus taught us to believe. The essence of this form of prayer transcends movements and names—it is a return to the knowing that we are already whole, already worthy, already held in Love.

One of my favorite quotes is from the Gospel of Thomas: "*If you bring forth what is within you, what you bring forth will save you. If you do not bring forth what is within you, what you do not bring forth will destroy you.*"

Why do we need Spiritual Mind Treatment today? Because the world is loud, and fear can be persuasive. Because many are still praying from pain rather than from presence. Because remembering the Truth of who we are is the path to real healing—not just for ourselves, but for the collective.

This practice is not bound by tradition. It is a living, breathing expression of faith in alignment. It invites us into the stillness where we remember: we are not here to fix ourselves. We are here to reveal what has never been broken.

This book offers you 40 days of gentle, powerful realignment through these treatments. May they help you hear your own voice again—your Higher Self whispering, "You are already Home."

"Jesus said, 'Know what is in front of your face,
and what is hidden from you will be disclosed to you.
For there is nothing hidden that will not be revealed.'"

A Journey of Transformation

Welcome to your sacred 40-day journey of spiritual awakening and inner transformation. This book is a companion for your Soul, an invitation to explore the infinite power within you through the practice of Spiritual Mind Treatment.

Each day offers a new opportunity to step deeper into your divine essence, gently dissolving limiting beliefs, expanding your consciousness, and aligning with the truth of who you are.

This practice is not bound to any religion or specific tradition. A Spiritual Mind Treatment is a universal approach to connecting with the Higher Mind, God, the Infinite Intelligence, Source, the I AM, the Infinite Source of love, wisdom, and creative power that flows through all existence. However you call this presence, the name is not what matters. What matters is your willingness to open your heart, embrace the truth of your being, and allow this practice to guide you home to yourself not just in moments of extreme needs but every day.

Over the next 40 days, each Spiritual Mind Treatment will focus on a unique aspect of transformation, building upon the previous day like steps on a sacred staircase. **You will start**

where you are, exactly as you are, and allow the words to gently uplift you. Even if a Spiritual Mind Treatment feels distant from your current reality — your ego-based reality, trust that every declaration of truth, when spoken from the heart, plants a seed in your consciousness. With time, these seeds bloom into new patterns of thought, perception, and being. These seeds are replacing old data in your personal database — your subconscious.

Approach this journey with curiosity, compassion, and an open mind. Let this book be a sanctuary where you meet your Self with love, rediscover your innate divinity, and remember that you are already whole, already worthy, already enough, already blessed.

Have a beautiful journey!

Why I Wrote This Book

I wrote this book as an offering of love and light for those seeking a deeper connection to their true 'Self'. My own spiritual journey has been one of learning about my ego and my Higher Self, of unraveling illusions, quieting the ego's voice controlling my mental space, and rediscovering the infinite wisdom and peace that resides within.

Through my work as a metaphysical practitioner, spiritual coach and guide, I have witnessed the profound impact that words of Truth can have on a person's heart and mind, and how speaking divine profound heartfelt affirmations can dissolve fear, inspire courage, and awaken the soul.

When I slowly speak aloud a Spiritual Mind Treatment that I have written, I always feel words coming up from my Soul here and there, and those mostly bring up tears of releasing what is ego-based and aligning me with my True Self.

It is my genuine desire that this book becomes a beacon for you, reminding you of your inherent divinity, strength, and capacity for transformation. I know how it feels to long for inner peace and clarity, to seek a practice that feels both grounding and elevating. Spiritual Mind Treatment has been one of those practices for me, and I feel called to share it with you in the hope that it brings as much light to your life as it has in mine.

This book is not about fixing what is broken, because you are not broken, we are not broken. That's the ego's misuse of knowledge making us think that we are. It is about remembering what has always been whole within you. My wish is that each treatment becomes a sacred key, unlocking doors within your consciousness and guiding you gently back to your heart where you can hear your own inner teacher.

Thank you for allowing me to walk this path with you.

Breathe In, let go of your ego-based thoughts and vision, see from your Soul, and **Love Out**!

Dr. Nathalie Turgeon Ph.D.

First, what is a *Spiritual Mind Treatment*?

Have you ever heard of Spiritual Mind Treatment? Do you know what it is and who uses it?

A Spiritual Mind Treatment is a form of affirmative prayer that focuses on aligning with your Divine Truth and the power of the Higher Mind to experience healing, clarity, or desired outcomes. It aligns with any spiritual practice and carries no specific religious connotation. It is for anyone seeking inner alignment, peace, and uplifting energy.

Each Spiritual Mind Treatment follows a powerful, intentional structure:

Recognition: Acknowledging the Infinite Source of wisdom and love, whatever your beliefs may be.

Unification: Aligning with your True essence beyond the ego-based mind, recognizing your oneness with this Divine Presence.

Realization: Declaring your awareness and releasing limiting beliefs, affirming the truth of your being and the desired transformation.

Gratitude: Expressing heartfelt gratitude for the alignment and transformation already unfolding, even when the ego-based mind cannot believe it nor see it.

Release: Surrendering the treatment into the Divine Law of creation, trusting that it is already done. What we see and experience is the result of what has been created in Consciousness.

This practice is not about pleading or hoping for change, it is about claiming the truth that already exists within you and allowing your consciousness to rise to meet it. It's about lifting up any ego veils allowing you to see beyond them. As you engage with each treatment, you invite your mind to relax, your heart to open, and your spirit to soar.

May this practice become a gentle, empowering guide as you walk the path of your 40-day transformation.

Let's step into the sacred together.

Note:

The words related to the structure are not meant to be read, but for you to see it, so when you will create your own spiritual mind treatment, your mind already knows how to structure it allowing a better flow.

Do not let your ego control the words. Whether you use the word God, Source, Divine Mind, Infinite Intelligence, Divine Intelligence, I AM, Light, Lord in your daily life… let them be the same pure Love energy beneath them all.

Day 1: Awakening to Truth

*"Nothing real can be threatened.
Nothing unreal exists. Herein lies the peace of God."*
— *A Course in Miracles*

Recognition: I recognize the Infinite Presence of Divine Truth, the eternal source of wisdom and love that flows through all life. This Truth is unshakable, unwavering, and ever-present, even when my intellect cannot comprehend and see it.

Unification: I know that this Divine Truth is not separate from me. I am one with the essence of pure Love and Infinite Intelligence. Every cell of my being vibrates with the presence of this sacred reality.

Realization: I awaken to the Truth of who I am, my essence. I release the beliefs and illusions of lack, fear, and separation. I am whole, complete, and always divinely guided. I see my life through the lens of divine perfection, not ego-based perfection, knowing that all things always align for my highest good.

Gratitude: I am deeply grateful for this continued awakening. I give thanks for the clarity, peace, and unwavering love that fills my heart as I remember my Divine nature stepping away from my ego-based mind.

Release: I release this Truth into the Universal Law, knowing it is already done. I step into my day fully aligned with the power of my awakened Spirit. I step into my day with the joy of knowing that I am not alone.

And so it is!

Day 2: Embracing Divine Love

"Teach only love, for that is what you are."
— A Course in Miracles

Recognition: I recognize the boundless presence of Divine Love, the purest force in existence. This Love is infinite, unconditional, and ever flowing. This pure unconditional Love is the foundation of all creation.

Unification: I know that this Divine Love is my essence. It pulses through my being, radiating from my heart. Flowing through me through each breath. I am not separate from Love; I am Love.

Realization: I embrace the truth that I am worthy of infinite Love. I release all the stories of unworthiness, all fears of rejection, all beliefs that keep me from fully receiving and expressing this unconditional Love. Love is not what my intellect defines. Love is my birthright. Love is my nature. Love is the truth of who I am.

Gratitude: My heart overflows with gratitude for the gift of Divine Love. I am thankful for the Love that surrounds me, even if my ego-based mind prefers to not see it, the Love that fills me, and the Love that I effortlessly share with the world.

Release: I release this treatment into the Infinite Universe, knowing that Divine Love is already active within me and my life. I walk through this day as a vessel of Love.

And so it is!

Day 3: Releasing Fear

> *"If you knew Who walks beside you on the way that you have chosen, fear would be impossible."*
> — *A Course in Miracles*

Recognition: I recognize the Infinite Presence of Divine Love, the boundless and unshakable Source of peace. This Presence is absolute, unwavering, and ever-present, holding all of creation in perfect safety. There is nothing outside of this Love, and within it, there is no fear.

Unification: I align myself with this truth. I open my heart and mind to the awareness that I am eternally safe in the embrace of Divine Love. Fear is not real—it is only a shadow, a passing illusion. I stand in the light of truth, where fear cannot exist.

I release every false belief that has given fear a place in my mind. I let go of the stories, doubts, and imagined limitations that have kept me small. I surrender all anxiety, worry, and hesitation into the hands of the Divine, where they dissolve into nothingness.

Realization: I declare that I am free. I walk forward with confidence, knowing that I am always guided, always supported, and always protected. I embrace life with trust, allowing love to be my guide. My heart is open, my mind is clear, and my spirit is strong.

Gratitude: I am grateful for the peace that fills me now, for the courage that rises within me, and for the unshakable truth that I am safe in the arms of Love. I give thanks that fear no longer holds power over me.

Release: I release this word into Divine Law, knowing that fear has no place in my being. Only Love remains.

And so it is!

Day 3: Releasing Fear and Embracing Peace

"There is nothing to fear."
— A Course in Miracles

Recognition: I recognize the presence of Divine Peace — an eternal stillness that exists beyond all appearances, untouched by the variations of the world.

Unification: I know that this Peace is within me and comes from me. It is not something I must seek anywhere else, but something I already am. I am one with the serene presence of the Divine.

Realization: I release all my ego-based fear in all its forms. I let go of anxious thoughts, imagined threats, and the heavy weight of what-ifs. Fear is an illusion. Fear is the opposite of Love, and I choose to return to the Peace that is my birthright and my essence.

Gratitude: I am profoundly grateful for the gift of inner Peace always present. I give thanks for the quiet strength it brings, the clarity it provides, and the unwavering calm that carries me through every experience.

Release: I release this treatment into the Divine, knowing that Peace is my reality now. I walk in serenity.

And so it is!

Day 4: Cultivating Inner Peace

*"Peace is the bridge that everyone will cross
to leave this world behind."
— A Course in Miracles*

Recognition: I recognize the Infinite Presence of Peace, the stillness that permeates all of existence, untouched by the variations of the external world. This Peace is eternal, unwavering, and always available to me.

Unification: I align myself with this sacred stillness, feeling my heart soften and my mind quiet as I rest in the embrace of divine tranquility. I breathe in this Peace, allowing it to flow through every part of my being, anchoring me in the present moment.

Realization: I release all thoughts of conflict, all inner turbulence, and all attachments to chaos or worry. I let go of the belief that Peace is something I must chase or earn, instead, I remember that Peace is my natural state, always within.
I declare that Peace reigns in my heart, that it flows through my words, my actions, and my presence. I become a beacon of calm, radiating serenity to the world around me.

Gratitude: I am grateful for the gift of inner Peace, for the knowing that no circumstance, no storm, can disturb the quiet sanctuary within my soul.

Release: I release this word into Divine Law, trusting that Peace is already established within me, now and always.

And so it is!

Day 5: Trusting the Divine Process

"I will step back and let Him lead the way."
— A Course in Miracles

Recognition: I recognize the Infinite Intelligence of the Divine, the perfect order and flow that governs all of life.

Unification: I align my heart with this sacred rhythm, knowing that I am always being guided, even when I cannot yet see the full picture. I breathe in trust, feeling the gentle assurance of divine orchestration.

Realization: I release all resistance, all impatience, and all doubt. I let go of the need to force, fix, or rush. I surrender to the divine unfolding, knowing every step is purposeful, and I am always in the right place at the right time.

I declare that I am divinely supported, that the path is being revealed moment by moment. I walk with grace, faith, and a quiet confidence that all is well.

Gratitude: I am grateful for the unseen blessings, for the synchronicities and signs that whisper, *"You are held."* I rejoice in the beauty of divine timing even if my ego-based mind cannot see it unfolding perfectly well.

Release: I release this word into the Law of Creation, trusting that everything is working together for my highest good.

And so it is!

Day 6: Remembering Your Worthiness

"You are altogether irreplaceable in the Mind of God."
— A Course in Miracles

Recognition: I recognize the Infinite Presence of Love, the Divine Source that created all life in perfect wholeness and radiance. This Love knows no conditions, no exceptions. It is pure, boundless, and eternal.

Unification: I align with this sacred Love, feeling it flowing through me like a gentle river, washing away any illusion of lack or unworthiness. I remember that I am an expression of the Divine, created in the image of perfection, inherently valuable simply because I exist.

Realization: I release the belief that I must prove myself, earn love, or seek validation outside of my being. I let go of every false story that tells me I am not enough, not doing enough. These illusions dissolve in the light of Truth.
I declare that I am worthy of love, joy, abundance, and every beautiful experience life offers. I honor my existence, knowing that my presence is meaningful and that my light contributes to the whole.

Gratitude: I am grateful for this remembrance, for the truth that my worth is unshakable and everlasting. I give thanks for the Love that surrounds me and fills me in every moment.

Release: I release this word into Divine Law, knowing it is already done.

And so it is

Day 7: Stepping into Gratitude

"Gratitude goes hand in hand with love, and where one is the other must be found."
— A Course in Miracles

Recognition: I recognize the Infinite Source of Abundance, the Divine Presence that pours endless blessings into my life. This Presence is the giver of all gifts — seen and unseen, constantly offering opportunities for growth, connection, and joy.

Unification: I align with the flow of gratitude, feeling my heart expand as I become aware of the countless blessings that already fill my life. I open my eyes to the beauty around me, the love that surrounds me, and the infinite possibilities that unfold with each breath.

Realization: I release the habit of focusing on what seems missing or lacking. I let go of any resistance to life as it is and surrender the need to control outcomes. In this surrender, I discover that gratitude transforms every experience, revealing the hidden treasures within even the most ordinary moments.

I declare that gratitude is my natural state. I choose to live with a thankful heart, appreciating the perfection of each day, the lessons of each challenge, and the miracles woven into every encounter.

Gratitude: I am grateful for the gift of awareness, for the realization that gratitude is not a fleeting emotion but a sacred way of being. I celebrate the joy that gratitude brings and the peace it cultivates within me.

Release: I release this word into Divine Law, knowing that my life is already overflowing with blessings.

And so it is!

Day 8: Aligning with Abundance

"To have, give all to all."
— A Course in Miracles

Recognition: I recognize the Infinite Source of Abundance, the ever-flowing presence of Divine Supply that knows no limits or restrictions. This Abundance is the very essence of creation, present in every blade of grass, every star in the sky, and every beat of my heart.

Unification: I align myself with this infinite flow, this natural infinite flow of well-being, knowing that I am one with the Divine Source. Abundance is not something I must seek — it is my birthright, an inherent part of my being. I open my heart to receive, trusting that all I need flows to me in perfect timing and perfect form.

Realization: I release every ego-based thought of scarcity, lack, or limitation separated from my natural infinite flow of well-being, of abundance. I let go of the belief that abundance is something outside of me or that I am unworthy of receiving it. Abundance is not something I must seek, but something I must align with. These illusions dissolve as I remember the Truth of who I am — a divine expression of infinite possibility.

I declare that abundance flows freely through every aspect of my life. I am abundant in love, creativity, wisdom, opportunities, and resources. I walk through life with an open heart, sharing my gifts and receiving the Universe's blessings with gratitude and ease.

Gratitude: I am grateful for the overflowing abundance that surrounds me, for the evidence of Divine Provision in every moment. I celebrate the endless ways the Universe supports and sustains me.

Release: I release this word into Divine Law, knowing that Abundance is already present in my life, here and now.

And so it is!

Day 9: Honoring Your Intuition

"The voice for God comes from your own altars to Him."
— A Course in Miracles

Recognition: I recognize the Infinite Wisdom that flows through all creation, the Divine Intelligence that speaks in gentle whispers and subtle nudges. This wisdom is always present, always guiding, and always seeking to lead me towards my highest good.

Unification: I align with this sacred inner voice, the quiet knowing that rises from the depths of my soul. I turn my attention inward, softening my mind and opening my heart to the divine messages that are always available to me. I trust that this inner guidance is a direct connection to the Divine.

Realization: I release the habit of doubting myself or seeking answers solely outside of me. I let go of the fear of making mistakes and the belief that I am disconnected from Divine Wisdom. These false ideas dissolve in the light of truth as I remember that intuition is my soul's language.

I declare that I am deeply connected to my inner wisdom. I honor the voice within me, trusting its insights and allowing it to lead me with love and clarity. Every decision I make is guided by Divine Intelligence, and I walk my path with confidence and grace.

Gratitude: I am grateful for the gift of intuition, for the constant companionship of Divine Wisdom within me. I give thanks for the peace and certainty that come from listening to my soul's voice and honoring my inner knowing.

Release: I release this word into Divine Law, knowing that my intuition is a sacred compass, always guiding me home to Truth.

And so it is!

Day 10: Healing Old Wounds

> *"Healing is accomplished the instant the sufferer no longer sees any value in pain."*
> — A Course in Miracles

Recognition: I recognize the Infinite Presence of Divine Love, the ever-compassionate Source that holds all things in wholeness. This Love knows no separation, no brokenness — only the eternal Truth of completeness and perfection.

Unification: I align with this Love, allowing it to fill every part of my being. I welcome its gentle light into the places within me that still carry pain, fear, or sorrow. I remember that I am not my wounds, but a divine being, whole and complete beyond all past experiences.

Realization: I release the grip of old stories and the illusion of being defined by past hurts. I let go of the belief that pain must linger, or that time is the healer. I surrender every lingering fragment of suffering into the hands of Divine Love, where it is transformed and dissolved.

I declare that healing is my natural state. I allow Love to flow freely through my heart, mending what once felt broken. I forgive myself and others, not to condone the past, but to free my spirit. I walk forward unburdened, embracing my inherent wholeness.

Gratitude: I am grateful for the gift of healing, for the infinite grace that allows me to release the past and step fully into the present. I give thanks for the strength, wisdom, and compassion that have blossomed from my experiences.

Release: I release this word into Divine Law, knowing that healing is already complete, and I am restored to peace.

And so it is!

Day 11: Expanding Consciousness

> *"Seek not to change the world, but choose to change your mind about the world."*
> — A Course in Miracles

Recognition: I recognize the Infinite Intelligence that is ever-expanding, limitless, and boundless. This Divine Presence is the Source of all wisdom, understanding, and awareness. It is the light that reveals Truth, the Love that dissolves illusion, and the power that awakens all beings to their highest potential. This Presence is everywhere, always expanding, always unfolding in perfect order.

Unification: I align with this Infinite Intelligence, knowing that it is not separate from me. It moves through me, as me, expanding my awareness in every moment. My consciousness is one with the Divine Mind, and I open myself fully to its wisdom. As I align with this greater truth, I step beyond the limitations of the ego and into the vastness of my true nature.

Realization: I release all barriers to growth, dissolving the false beliefs that have kept my mind confined. I embrace clarity, divine wisdom, and higher understanding. I open my heart and mind to expanded perception, seeing beyond appearances into the deeper reality of Love and Oneness. Every moment, my consciousness evolves, my awareness deepens, and my understanding expands.

Gratitude: I am profoundly grateful for this awakening, for the limitless possibilities that unfold before me. I give thanks for the expansion of my mind, the deepening of my wisdom, and the clarity that now fills my being. I rejoice in the knowing that I am forever evolving, forever unfolding in divine perfection.

Release: I release this word into Divine Law, knowing that the expansion of my consciousness is already happening. I trust in the divine unfolding of my awareness, knowing that I am always guided into greater truth.

And so it is!

Day 12: Seeing with Spiritual Vision

*"The body's eyes see only form.
The spiritual eye sees only truth."*
— A Course in Miracles

Recognition: I recognize the Divine Presence as the Source of all true vision. This Infinite Intelligence sees beyond illusion, beyond appearance, beyond the shifting forms of the world. It perceives only Truth, only Love, only the eternal reality of wholeness and perfection. In the Light of Divine Awareness, all things are seen as they truly are.

Unification: I align myself with this higher vision, knowing that my spiritual sight is one with the sight of the Divine. I do not need to rely on the limited perception of the physical eyes, for I am given the ability to see beyond—to perceive with the eyes of love, clarity, and wisdom. My spiritual vision is clear, unclouded by fear or judgment.

Realization: I release all illusions, all distortions of perception that have kept me bound to the false. I surrender the habit of seeing through the lens of separation, lack, or limitation. I open myself to a greater reality—one where Love is all-encompassing, where Truth is unmistakable, and where the Divine is revealed in all things.

Gratitude: I give thanks for this expanded vision, for the clarity and wisdom that now guide me. I rejoice in the knowing that I see rightly and that I witness the world through the lens of love and divine understanding. I am grateful that my perception is aligned with Truth.

Release: I release this word into Divine Law, knowing that my spiritual sight is already perfected. I trust in the unfolding of my vision, in the revelation of Truth in every moment.

And so it is.

Day 13: Letting Go of Control

"I will step back and let Him lead the way."
— A Course in Miracles

Recognition: I recognize the Infinite Presence of Divine Intelligence, the ever-flowing, all-knowing Source that orchestrates all of life with perfect harmony. This Presence moves with grace, effortlessly unfolding creation in divine order. Nothing is forced, nothing is grasped, everything is guided by the rhythm of Love, unfolding as it should.

Unification: I align myself with this divine flow, knowing that I am not separate from it. The same Intelligence that governs the stars, the tides, and the seasons moves through me. I no longer need to control, to force, or to struggle. Instead, I surrender to the infinite wisdom that is already leading me, supporting me, and working through me.

Realization: I release the illusion that I must control life for things to go well. I let go of the need to grasp, resist, or manipulate outcomes. I surrender my plans, my worries, my need to figure everything out. I trust that life is unfolding perfectly, even when I do not yet see the full picture. I embrace the truth that I am always guided, always supported, and always exactly where I need to be.

Gratitude: I give thanks for the peace that fills me now. I am grateful for the freedom that comes with trust, the lightness that comes with surrender. I rejoice in the knowing that I do not walk this path alone, and I celebrate the divine orchestration that is always at work in my life.

Release: I release this word into Divine Law, knowing that my surrender is met with grace. I trust, I let go, I allow.

And so it is!

Day 14: Welcoming Miracles

"Miracles are natural. When they do not occur, something has gone wrong."
— A Course in Miracles

Recognition: I recognize the ever-present Reality of Divine Love, the limitless Source from which all miracles arise. This Presence knows no lack, no limitation, no obstacles—only the boundless unfolding of truth, grace, and perfect harmony. Miracles are not exceptions; they are the natural expression of Divine Love in action.

Unification: I am one with this miraculous Presence. I am not separate from the divine flow, nor am I bound by the illusions of time, space, or difficulty. The same love that heals, restores, and transforms moves through me, in me, and as me. Miracles are my inheritance, for they are the natural state of being when I align with truth. Miracles are course-correction of my beliefs and thoughts in Consciousness.

Realization: I now release all resistance to miracles. I let go of doubts, fears, and the false belief that I must struggle or strive. I welcome the effortless unfolding of divine order in my life. I open my heart and mind to see as Spirit sees, to trust as Love trusts, and to receive as freely as I give. Miracles are here, now, always available. I accept them fully.

Gratitude: I give thanks for the certainty that miracles are already present in my life. I rejoice in the quiet knowing that I need not force, earn, or prove anything—only welcome, only allow. I am grateful for the peace that comes from remembering the Truth: Love is my reality, and miracles flow freely where Love is recognized.

Release: I release this word into Divine Law, trusting that miracles unfold effortlessly in perfect ways beyond my comprehension. I let go. I trust. I receive.

And so it is!

Day 15: Strengthening Inner Resilience

"Nothing real can be threatened. Nothing unreal exists. Herein lies the peace of God."
— A Course in Miracles

Recognition: I recognize the infinite strength of the Divine, the unwavering Presence that is the foundation of all life. This Presence is unshaken, eternal, and limitless. It is the source of all courage, all wisdom, and all resilience. In the face of any challenge, this Divine Power remains steady, for it is Love itself, and Love cannot be broken.

Unification: I align myself with this sacred strength, knowing that I am not separate from it. The same unshakable presence that moves the stars and calms the storm dwells within me. I am not weak, for I am an extension of the Divine. I do not stand alone. I am supported, uplifted, and carried by the infinite wisdom and power of Spirit.

Realization: I release all belief in fragility, doubt, and limitation. I awaken to the truth that I am resilient, not because of my own will, but because I am anchored in Divine Love. No situation, no fear, no external condition can shake the truth of who I am. I rise above appearances, knowing that within me is an infinite wellspring of courage, peace, and inner fortitude.

Gratitude: I give thanks for the strength that is already present within me. I am grateful that, no matter what arises, I can return to the quiet knowing that I am held, supported, and empowered by Divine Truth. I celebrate the resilience that flows through me, allowing me to meet each moment with faith, clarity, and grace.

Release: I release this word into the Law of Creation, trusting that my inner resilience is deepened and strengthened in perfect and miraculous ways. I let go, I trust, and I allow.

And so it is!

Day 16: Forgiving Yourself and Others

> *"Forgiveness recognizes what you thought your brother did to you has not occurred."*
> — A Course in Miracles

Recognition: I recognize the Divine as the Infinite Presence of Love, the essence of true forgiveness. This Love holds no grievances, no condemnation, no separation. It is pure, ever-present, and whole. In this Divine Truth, there is only peace, only unity, only freedom.

Unification: I align myself with this sacred Love, knowing that I am one with it. The same divine light that forgives, restores, and makes all things new flows through me now. There is no part of me separate from this Love, and there is no part of another that is separate from it either. We are all embraced in the wholeness of Divine Truth.

Realization: I now release all burdens of judgment, guilt, and resentment. I recognize that holding onto grievances only binds me to illusions of pain and separation. In Truth, I am already free, and so is everyone else. I forgive myself for believing in mistakes, and I forgive others for what I once perceived as harm. I choose to see through the eyes of Spirit, where only love is real.

Gratitude: I give thanks for this deep liberation. I celebrate the peace that flows through me as I open my heart to love once more. I am grateful for the healing that forgiveness brings, for the lightness of being that fills me as I release all that no longer serves. Love is all there is, and I am thankful to remember this truth.

Release: I release this word into the Divine Law, knowing that forgiveness has already taken place. I let go of the past and step fully into the now, where only Love remains.

And so it is!

Day 17: Anchoring in Present Moment Awareness

"Be still, and know that I am God."
— Psalm 46:10

Recognition: I recognize the Divine as the ever-present Now—the stillness beyond thought, the peace that exists in this very moment. Spirit is not found in the past nor the future but in the eternal now, where all things are whole, perfect, and complete. This Presence is life itself, unfolding in infinite wisdom, beauty, and grace.

Unification: I align myself with this sacred Presence, knowing that I am one with it. There is no separation between me and the Divine flow of life. I am not lost in yesterday or waiting for tomorrow. I am here, now, fully present in the embrace of Spirit. The breath of the Divine moves through me, reminding me that I am always exactly where I need to be.

Realization: I release all distractions, all worries, all attachments to time. I awaken to the stillness within me, to the awareness that all is well in this moment. I trust that everything I need is available to me now. I am anchored in the present, where clarity, peace, and divine guidance are always available. As I rest in this moment, I am fully alive, fully awake, fully in tune with the perfection of now.

Gratitude: I give thanks for the gift of presence, for the deep knowing that I am supported in every breath, in every heartbeat. I celebrate the peace that fills me as I surrender to the now. I am grateful for the awareness that life is unfolding perfectly, and I embrace this moment with an open heart.

Release: I release this word into Divine Law, trusting that my awareness deepens, my presence strengthens, and my spirit remains anchored in the Now. I let go, I trust, I breathe.

And so it is!

Day 18: Embodying Self-Love

*"You are altogether irreplaceable in the Mind of God.
No one else can fill your part."*
— *A Course in Miracles*

Recognition: I recognize the Divine as the infinite, unconditional Love that has no beginning and no end. This Love is pure, unshakable, and ever-present. It is the very essence of life itself, flowing through all that is. Spirit does not withhold love, nor does it judge—it simply radiates as perfect wholeness, embracing all creation in complete acceptance.

Unification: I align with this sacred Love, for I am one with it. There is no part of me that is separate from Divine Love. As I open my heart, I realize that the same love that created the stars, the oceans, and the mountains is the love that created me. I am a perfect expression of the Divine, whole and worthy exactly as I am.

Realization: I now release all illusions of unworthiness, all false beliefs that tell me I am not enough. I no longer seek love outside of myself, for I recognize that Love is already within me. I embrace myself fully—the light and the shadow, the beauty and the ego-based imperfection—knowing that all of me is held in Divine Love. As I honor my true essence, I treat myself with kindness, compassion, and reverence. I speak to myself with gentleness, I nourish my body, mind, and spirit, and I trust in my divine worth.

Gratitude: I give thanks for the deep knowing that I am loved, not for what I do, but simply because I am. I celebrate the freedom that comes from embracing my true Self. I am grateful for the Love that flows through me and as me, blessing my life in every way.

Release: I release this word into Divine Law, trusting that self-love is not something I must earn, but something I already am. I let go, I trust, I embody this Truth.

And so it is!

Day 19: Radiating Compassion

*"As I see him, I will see myself. As I treat him,
I will treat myself. As I think of him, I will think of myself.
In him, I find my Self, or lose myself."*
— A Course in Miracles

Recognition: I recognize the Divine as the ever-present Love that moves through all of existence. This Love is infinite, boundless, and without condition. It flows as compassion, understanding, and grace, touching all beings, all hearts, all souls. In this Divine Presence, there is no separation—only unity, only Love expressing Itself in infinite ways.

Unification: I align myself with this sacred Love, knowing that I am one with it. As the Divine is compassionate, so too am I. As the Divine sees all with unconditional understanding, so too do I open my heart to see beyond appearances, beyond fears, beyond illusion. Compassion is not outside of me; it is the truth of who I am.

Realization: I now release any barriers that block the full expression of compassion through me. I let go of judgment, impatience, or resistance, and I allow the gentle presence of Love to flow freely from my heart. I see with eyes of understanding, I listen with a heart of kindness, and I meet all beings, including myself, with gentleness and care. My words, my actions, my very presence radiate the compassion of the Divine. Wherever I go, Love goes with me.

Gratitude: I give thanks for the limitless well of compassion within me, for the ability to bring peace, healing, and comfort to those around me. I am grateful for the Love that flows through me, for the way my presence can uplift and soothe others. I celebrate this truth and welcome even greater expressions of Divine compassion in my life.

Release: I release this word into Divine Law, knowing that it is already done. Compassion flows through me effortlessly, naturally, abundantly. I let go, I trust, I radiate Love.

And so it is!

Day 20: Affirming Divine Order

"There is no chaos in God's plan."
— A Course in Miracles

Recognition: I recognize the Divine as the Infinite Intelligence that governs all of existence. There is an order so vast, so perfect, that every star remains in its place, every wave follows its rhythm, and every breath moves in harmony with life itself. This Divine Order is not random; it is the sacred flow of the Universe, unfolding with absolute precision and purpose.

Unification: I align myself with this Divine Order, knowing that it is the very essence of my being. Just as the sun rises each day without struggle, so too does my life unfold according to a Higher Intelligence. There is no separation between me and the perfect flow of the Universe—I am within it, and it is within me.

Realization: I now release any illusion of disorder, chaos, or uncertainty. I let go of resistance, knowing that everything in my life is unfolding exactly as it should. Even when my limited vision from my ego-based mind cannot see the full picture, I trust that Divine Order is always at work, bringing clarity, alignment, and balance into every area of my life.

Gratitude: I give thanks for this perfect alignment, for the knowing that I am always supported, always guided, always in the right place at the right time. I am grateful that every step I take is part of a greater plan that serves my highest good. With a heart full of peace, I embrace this Truth.

Release: I release this word into the Infinite Law, knowing that Divine Order is already established. I surrender fully, trusting that all is well, and all is unfolding in harmony.

And so it is!

Day 21: Embracing Change

"Change is always fearful to the separated, because they cannot conceive of it as a move towards healing the separation."
— *A Course in Miracles*

Recognition: I recognize the Divine as the ever-flowing, ever-evolving Presence that moves through all of life. Just as the seasons change, just as the tides rise and fall, so too does the movement of the Infinite shape and expand all creation. This Divine Intelligence is not stagnant—it is alive, dynamic, and forever unfolding in perfect harmony.

Unification: I align myself with this sacred flow, knowing that I am one with the Divine movement of life. I am not separate from change—I am an expression of it. Every breath, every moment, every experience is part of my soul's expansion. The same Intelligence that orchestrates the Universe orchestrates my path, ensuring that all change leads me towards greater wholeness and awakening.

Realization: I release any fear, resistance, or hesitation surrounding change. I no longer cling to what was or fear what will be—I stand firmly in the present, trusting that each shift is an opportunity for growth, expansion, and deepened awareness. Change is not happening *to* me; it is happening *for* me, always leading me into greater alignment with my highest good.

Gratitude: I give thanks for the transformation unfolding in my life. I welcome new possibilities, fresh perspectives, and unseen blessings. I am grateful for the wisdom that allows me to embrace change with openness, knowing that each step is divinely guided.

Release: I surrender this truth into the Infinite Law, knowing that all is unfolding as it should. I trust, I flow, I embrace change with a heart full of peace.

And so it is!

Day 22: Releasing Limiting Stories

"The truth is true, and nothing else is true."
— *A Course in Miracles*

Recognition: I recognize the Divine as the eternal source of Truth, the boundless field of limitless possibility. There are no restrictions in the Infinite; there is only expansion, love, and the pure essence of creation. This Divine Presence is not bound by the past, nor confined by human stories, it simply *is*, whole and free.

Unification: I align myself with this eternal Truth, knowing that I, too, am limitless. I am not defined by old narratives, past experiences, or conditioned beliefs. The same creative power that moves galaxies moves through me, and I am free to choose a new reality at any moment.

Realization: I now release every story that tells me I am small, unworthy, incapable, or bound by limitation. These are illusions, echoes of an unhealed mind, and they hold no power over me. I see them for what they are—shadows of the past, and I allow them to dissolve in the radiant light of Truth. I am not my past. I am not my old wounds. I am not the falsehoods I once believed. I am a divine being, whole, free, and infinitely capable.

Gratitude: I give thanks for this newfound clarity, for the liberation of my mind, and for the Truth that sets me free. I am grateful for the power within me to rewrite my story, to step into my highest expression, and to live in alignment with my divine nature.

Release: I release these words into the Infinite, knowing that my transformation is already complete. I let go, I trust, I walk forward unburdened and renewed.

And so it is!

Day 23: Calling in Joy

"Joy is unlimited, because each shining thought of love extends its being and creates more of itself."
— A Course in Miracles

Recognition: I recognize the Divine as the source of infinite joy, a wellspring of radiant light that knows no bounds. Joy is not something to be sought, it is the very nature of the Divine. It moves through creation as the laughter of the Universe, the song of the soul, the dance of life unfolding in perfect harmony.

Unification: I align myself with this sacred Joy, knowing that it is not separate from me. It is not something outside of me, nor something I must earn. Joy is my birthright, my natural state, my essence as an extension of the Divine. As the sun cannot help but shine, I cannot help but be Joy, for I am one with the light of the Infinite.

Realization: I now release all that dims my inner radiance. I let go of burdens, doubts, and fears that have veiled the Joy that is already within me. I no longer wait for circumstances to grant me happiness—I *am* Joy in this moment. I embrace laughter, ease, and delight as sacred expressions of my divine nature. Joy is here, now, alive in me!

Gratitude: With a heart overflowing, I give thanks for this truth. I rejoice in the knowing that Joy is always present, always accessible, always mine to embrace. I am grateful for every moment of delight, every spark of lightness, and the endless ways Joy manifests in my life.

Release: I release these words into the Divine Law, knowing that the presence of Joy flows effortlessly through me now and always. I open my heart, I welcome it fully, and I allow Divine Joy to lead the way.

And so it is!

Day 24: Deepening Faith

> *"Faith is the opposite of fear, as much a part of love*
> *as fear is of attack."*
> — A Course in Miracles

Recognition: I recognize the Divine as the unwavering presence of love, wisdom, and certainty. It is the unshakable foundation upon which all things rest, the steady current that carries all of life forward in perfect order. In the Infinite, there is no doubt, no hesitation—only the certainty of Truth, the fullness of love, and the assurance of divine grace.

Unification: I align myself with this boundless Presence, knowing that I am never separate from it. The faith of the Divine is my faith, the trust of the Universe is my trust. I let go of the illusion of separation and remember that I am eternally supported, divinely guided, and deeply held in the embrace of Spirit.

Realization: I now release all doubts, all fears, all questioning of the Divine's presence in my life. Faith is not something I must strive for—it is already within me, as natural as the beating of my heart. I trust in the unseen, in the unfolding of my path, in the wisdom that orchestrates all things for the highest good. I know that even when I do not see the full picture, I am being led with love, and I walk forward with confidence and peace.

Gratitude: I give thanks for this deepening faith, for the knowing that I am safe, supported, and always exactly where I need to be. I rejoice in the certainty that life is unfolding perfectly, that the Divine is ever-present, and that I am held in Infinite Love.

Release: I release these words into the Divine Mind, knowing that faith is already anchored within me. I trust, I surrender, and I rest in the peace of knowing that all is well.

And so it is!

Day 25: Uncovering Inner Wisdom

> *"The quiet center, where you do not change and where you cannot be changed, remains untouched by all the ego's frantic attempts to obscure your reality."*
> — A Course in Miracles

Recognition: I recognize the Divine as the source of Infinite Wisdom, the timeless intelligence that flows through all creation. It is the knowing beyond words, the clarity beyond reason, the Truth that remains steady and unshaken. This Wisdom is the essence of all that is, ever-present and ever-guiding.

Unification: I align myself with this Divine Wisdom, knowing that it is not separate from me. It is not something outside of me that I must seek—it is the very core of my being. As a wave is one with the ocean, so too am I one with the all-knowing presence of Spirit.

Realization: I now release all illusions of confusion, doubt, and uncertainty. I let go of the belief that I do not know or that the answers lie beyond my reach. The Truth has always been within me, waiting in the stillness. I choose now to listen, to trust, to open my heart and mind to the divine whispers that arise from within. With each breath, I sink deeper into my inner knowing, allowing Wisdom to flow effortlessly through me.

Gratitude: With deep appreciation, I give thanks for this ever-present Wisdom that guides my life with love and clarity. I rejoice in the knowing that every answer I seek is already within me, ready to be revealed at the perfect time. I am grateful for the ease, the confidence, and the peace that comes from trusting my inner guidance.

Release: I release these words into the Divine Mind, knowing that Wisdom is already unfolding within me. I let go, I trust, and I walk forward in certainty.

And so it is!

Day 26: Aligning with Your Purpose

> *"Your function in Heaven is creation.
> Your function on earth is healing."*
> — A Course in Miracles

Recognition: I recognize the Divine as the grand orchestrator of life, the Infinite Intelligence that weaves purpose into every soul. There is no randomness, no mistake—only perfect design, unfolding in divine order. Purpose is not separate from Spirit; it is Spirit expressing Itself through all things, guiding each being to their highest calling.

Unification: I align with this truth, knowing that I am not lost, nor am I without purpose. I am an expression of the Divine, a vessel through which love, wisdom, and creativity flow. My purpose is already within me, woven into the fabric of my being. As I open myself to divine guidance, I allow my path to be revealed with clarity and ease.

Realization: I now release all doubts, fears, and illusions that tell me I do not know my purpose or that I must struggle to find it. Purpose is not something I must chase—it is something I allow. It reveals itself in the quiet spaces, in the moments when I listen to my heart, in the things that bring me joy and light me up from within. I trust that I am already on the path of my highest calling, and as I step forward in faith, all is made clear.

Gratitude: I am deeply grateful for the divine purpose that flows through me. I give thanks for the clarity, the confidence, and the trust that fills my heart. I celebrate the unique way Spirit expresses Itself through me, knowing that my presence in this world is meaningful and needed.

Release: I release these words into the Infinite Mind, knowing that my purpose is already unfolding perfectly. I let go of striving, I surrender to divine guidance, and I walk forward with peace and certainty.

And so it is!

Day 27: Claiming Your True Power

> *"Nothing real can be threatened. Nothing unreal exists. Herein lies the peace of God."*
> — A Course in Miracles

Recognition: I recognize the Divine as the source of all true power. This power is not force, nor is it control—it is the infinite presence of Love, the unshakable truth of my being. It is the essence that moves mountains, heals wounds, and restores peace. This power is always present, never wavering, and available to all who align with it.

Unification: I align with this divine power now. It is not separate from me; it flows through me, as me. I am one with the limitless presence of God, and therefore, I am strong, whole, and complete. My true power is not found in external things, nor in the illusions of the world, but in my divine inheritance as a creation of Love Itself.

Realization: I now release all beliefs that tell me I am weak, incapable, or lacking. These are mere illusions of the ego, and they hold no truth in the light of my divine being. I claim my power as a conscious creator, as one who walks in alignment with truth, grace, and purpose. I no longer look outside myself for validation—I stand firm in the knowing that I am supported, guided, and empowered from within.

Gratitude: With a heart full of gratitude, I give thanks for this power that flows through me. I am thankful for the courage, wisdom, and love that rise within me, guiding my every step. I rejoice in the freedom that comes from embracing my true essence, and I honor the divine strength that is mine to express in this world.

Release: I release these words into the vast and Infinite Law of creation, knowing they are already fulfilled. I let go, I trust, and I walk forward in the full embodiment of my true power.

And so it is!

Day 28: Trusting Divine Timing

"Those who are certain of the outcome can afford to wait, and wait without anxiety."
— A Course in Miracles

Recognition: I recognize the Divine as the orchestrator of all things, the Infinite Intelligence that weaves the perfect unfolding of life. There are no mistakes, no delays—only the divine order of Love working for the highest good. Time itself is held within this sacred wisdom, moving in perfect harmony with all creation.

Unification: I align with this truth now. I am not separate from Divine Intelligence; I am a part of its perfect flow. Just as the stars shine in their appointed time, and the seasons change in divine rhythm, so too does my life unfold in absolute perfection. I trust that all is happening exactly as it should.

Realization: I release the illusion of urgency, the fear of delay, and the need to control outcomes. There is no need for impatience, for I am held in divine grace. What is meant for me cannot be missed, and what is not for me will effortlessly fall away. I trust that every step, every pause, and every moment of waiting is serving my highest good.

Gratitude: With a heart full of gratitude, I give thanks for the divine timing that guides my path. I celebrate the wisdom that unfolds my life in ways far greater than I could ever imagine. I am grateful for every moment—both the waiting and the receiving, knowing that all is well.

Release: I release this word into the Infinite Law of creation, knowing it is already fulfilled. I let go of worry, surrender to the flow, and rest in the peace of divine timing.

And so it is!

'Certainty' is... I walk in peace every day because I know who walks with me. I do not need to ego-see the final shape of the dream, the result, in my physical life because I know it is real, and I have seen it in "reality". I keep choosing to stay aligned with this dream every day and align with my Higher Self through what keeps me aligned as my day unfolds. This is my certainty in Spirit where my ego is not. This is me aligning with being certain of the outcome being present in my now, seeing my outcome in reality and not in ego-reality. My certainty was never to be found in my physical life, but in my reality, in Consciousness. Not backing away from our dream is certainty.

Day 29: Cultivating Boundless Creativity

"There is no limit to the Mind except those you place upon it."
— A Course in Miracles

Recognition: I recognize the Divine as the infinite source of all creation, the boundless wellspring of inspiration that flows through all life. Every masterpiece, every idea, every expression of beauty and wisdom is born from this sacred source. Creativity is not limited, for it is the very essence of life itself, forever expanding, forever renewing.

Unification: I align with this infinite creative power, knowing it moves through me effortlessly. I am one with divine inspiration, and my mind is an open channel for Its expression. There are no blocks, no limits—only the vast, limitless field of possibility. Creativity is not something outside of me; it is the very truth of who I am.

Realization: I now release any doubts, fears, or beliefs that would limit my creative flow. I let go of perfectionism, comparison, and hesitation. My creativity is unique, divinely guided, and meant to be expressed. I trust in the ideas that come to me, knowing they are gifts from the Higher Self. I allow creativity to pour through me with ease, joy, and purpose.

Gratitude: With a heart full of gratitude, I celebrate the infinite creativity that moves through me. I am thankful for the inspiration, the ideas, and the courage to bring them into form. I rejoice in the process of creation itself, knowing that every expression is a reflection of Divine Intelligence.

Release: I release this truth into the Divine Law, knowing that my creative flow is unblocked, unlimited, and ever-expanding. I trust that all I need to create is already within me. I surrender and allow the magic to unfold.

And so it is!

Day 30: Dissolving Doubt

"Doubt will vanish as I recognize that Spirit never fails."
— *A Course in Miracles*

Recognition: I recognize the Divine as absolute certainty, the unwavering presence of truth, love, and wisdom. In the Mind of the Infinite, there is no hesitation, no uncertainty, perfect knowing. The Divine is steadfast, whole, and complete, guiding all things with precision and love.

Unification: I align myself now with this divine certainty. There is no separation between me and the wisdom of the Infinite. I am one with Divine Intelligence, and within me exists the same unshakable Truth. I am grounded in the knowing that I am always supported, always guided, always safe in the arms of Divine Wisdom.

Realization: I release all doubt now. Any lingering hesitation, fear, or uncertainty dissolves in the light of divine Truth. I no longer question my worth, my path, or my ability to receive guidance. I trust in my inner knowing, for it is the voice of Spirit speaking through me. Every step I take is held in divine order.

Gratitude: I give thanks for the deep peace that comes with trust. I celebrate the clarity that fills my mind and heart. I am grateful for the wisdom that moves through me, the certainty that strengthens me, and the Divine Presence that assures me all is well.

Release: I now release this word into the Infinite Law of creation. Doubt dissolves completely, leaving only faith, confidence, and clarity. I trust in divine timing, Divine Wisdom, and divine love.

And so it is!

Day 31: Living in Reverence

> *"The holiest of all the spots on earth is where an ancient hatred has become a present love."*
> — A Course in Miracles

Recognition: I recognize the Divine as the Sacred Presence that moves through all things. Every breath, every moment, every particle of existence is infused with Divine Intelligence and Love. The Universe is not random, is holy, purposeful, and filled with grace. In this awareness, I bow in deep reverence to the sacred essence of all life.

Unification: I am one with this Divine Presence. The same sacred force that moves galaxies and births stars lives within me. I am not separate from the holiness of existence—I am an expression of it. With this truth, I align myself with the infinite beauty and wisdom that surrounds me, knowing I am a vessel of Divine Love.

Realization: I now open my heart to live in reverence. I choose to see the Divine in all things—the sun rising, the laughter of a child, the stillness of the night, the lessons hidden in every experience. My steps become sacred, my words become blessings, my actions become offerings of Love. I honor all life as a reflection of the Divine, and in doing so, I elevate my presence in the world.

Gratitude: With a heart overflowing, I give thanks for the deep awareness that fills me now. I am grateful for the gift of this sacred life, for the wisdom that allows me to walk in reverence, and for the divine grace that flows endlessly through me and all things.

Release: I release this word into the Infinite Law of creation, knowing that reverence is now the foundation of my being. I trust that as I walk in awareness of the sacred, life mirrors that holiness back to me.

And so it is!

Day 32: Remembering Unity Consciousness

"When you meet anyone, remember it is a holy encounter. As you see him, you will see yourself. As you treat him, you will treat yourself. As you think of him, you will think of yourself. Never forget this, for in him you will find yourself or lose yourself."
— A Course in Miracles

Recognition: I recognize the One Divine Presence that flows through all things. This presence is love, wisdom, and Infinite Intelligence, expressing Itself in countless forms. There is no separation—only unity, only wholeness. The Divine is everywhere, in everyone, and in everything.

Unification: I am one with this Infinite Presence. There is no space where I end and another begins, for we are all interconnected waves in the vast ocean of Divine Being. My essence is woven into the fabric of all creation, eternally united with all of life. What I think, feel, and do ripples into the whole, for we are One.

Realization: I now awaken to Unity Consciousness. I dissolve the illusion of separation and remember the truth: there is no "other." Each soul I encounter is a reflection of the Divine, just as I am. In this awareness, I choose love over judgment, peace over division, and connection over isolation. I see with the eyes of Oneness, honoring the sacred light in all beings.

Gratitude: With deep appreciation, I give thanks for this remembrance. I am grateful for the interconnectedness of all life, for the knowing that I am never alone, and for the love that binds us all together in sacred unity. This truth fills my heart and expands my being.

Release: I release this word into the Infinite Law of creation, knowing that unity is already the eternal reality. I surrender all false beliefs of separation and step fully into the awareness of Oneness.

And so it is!

Day 33: Blessing Your Relationships

"You are altogether irreplaceable in the Mind of God. No one else can fill your part in it. And while you leave your part of it empty, your eternal place merely waits for your return."
— *A Course in Miracles*

Recognition: I recognize the One Infinite Love that is the source and substance of all relationships. It is the Divine Presence that breathes life into connection, intimacy, and unity. Love is the foundation of all relating, whether seen or unseen, spoken or silent, near or distant. Every relationship is a sacred classroom for remembering God's Love.

Unification: I am one with this Divine Presence. The same Love that created me flows through every person I know, have known, or will ever meet. There is no separation between myself and the souls with whom I walk this path. We are each facets of the One Light, playing unique roles in each other's unfolding.

Realization: I now bless all my relationships—past, present, and future. I see them as holy, not because they were perfect in form, but because they served a higher purpose. I release all grievances and invite grace into every connection. I recognize that each soul encounter, no matter how brief or long, holds an invitation to grow in compassion, forgiveness, and love. I honor the teachers, the mirrors, the allies, and even the challengers—each one playing their sacred role in my awakening. I open my heart to the healing of every relationship, trusting that Divine Intelligence is working through them all.

Gratitude: I give thanks for the gift of every relationship. For the love shared, the lessons learned, and the ways I was guided closer to my True Self. I am grateful for the opportunity to love and be loved, to forgive and be forgiven, to witness and be witnessed in the light of truth. Thank you, Spirit, for blessing these sacred bonds.

Release: I release this treatment into the Infinite creative Law, knowing the blessings have already begun. Divine order governs my relationships, and Love goes before me to prepare the way. I surrender and trust

And so it is!

Day 34: Releasing Judgment

> "You have no idea of the tremendous release
> and deep peace that comes from meeting yourself
> and your brothers totally without judgment."
> — *A Course in Miracles*

Recognition: I recognize the One Infinite Presence, the Pure Light of Divine Intelligence, which sees only through the eyes of Love. This Presence holds no judgment, no condemnation—only the perfect knowing of what is eternally whole, innocent, and complete.

Unification: I am one with this Presence. The Mind that sees me in my wholeness is the same Mind that resides within me. I am not separate from Divine Love—I am Its expression. And because I am one with It, I have access to that same loving perception.

Realization: In this holy moment, I release judgment—of myself, of others, of circumstances. I surrender the ego's tendency to categorize, compare, and critique. I no longer seek to define what is right or wrong, good or bad, worthy or unworthy. Instead, I open to the deeper vision of the Holy Spirit within me—the one that sees beyond appearances and into Truth. I embrace the knowing that each soul is walking a sacred path, unfolding in perfect alignment with their divine curriculum. Judgment dissolves in the light of understanding.

Gratitude: I am grateful for the inner shift now occurring. I am grateful to remember that I can choose peace over judgment, love over fear. I give thanks for the spaciousness that fills my heart as I lay down the heavy burden of criticism. I am Light. I am free.

Release: I release this prayer into the loving, intelligent flow of Divine Law. I trust that this intention is already fulfilled. My heart is open. My mind is renewed. My eyes see with love.

And so it is!

Day 35: Honoring Your Body as Sacred

"The body is merely part of your experience in the physical world. Its abilities can be and are oversensitized. You do not need it at all in the Holy Instant. Learn to be quiet in the instant, and the truth is revealed to you."
— A Course in Miracles

Recognition: There is One Source of life—divine, infinite, and eternal. This Presence is not confined by form, yet it animates all of life through form. It is the Great I AM, the changeless Essence that expresses in infinite ways, including through the appearance of this body.

Unification: I am one with this Presence, with this Holy Consciousness that lives beyond the physical. I remember that my True Self is not the body but the eternal Spirit that gently uses the body as a means of expression, of giving and receiving Love. The body is not my identity—it is a sacred servant of the Divine when I surrender it to Higher Purpose.

Realization: In this holy recognition, I bless my body as sacred—not because it is who I am, but because it serves the Light within me. I choose to honor it with kindness, with gentle care, with rest, nourishment, movement, and reverence—not out of worship, but from devotion to the Truth that flows through me. My body is not something to be worshiped. It is a means to listen to the Divine. I see my hands, my voice, my breath, my presence—as instruments of healing, compassion, and grace. I no longer use the body to prove or protect the ego, but to extend peace, stillness, and Love into the world.

Gratitude: I give deep thanks for the holy function of this body—to reflect and radiate the consciousness of Truth. I am grateful for the ways it allows me to connect, to serve, to embody Light. I am grateful that it does not define me, limit me, or contain me. I honor the vessel, while I remain rooted in the Essence.

Release: With full trust, I release this awareness into the creative Law of Divine Mind. I step forward in Love, no longer confusing form with identity, but walking in sacred remembrance.

And so it is!

Day 36: Inviting Playfulness and Lightheartedness

"Into eternity, where all is one, there crept a tiny, mad idea, at which the Son of God remembered not to laugh."
— A Course in Miracles

Recognition: There is One Infinite Presence—Divine Intelligence, creative joy, the Source of all light, love, and laughter. This Presence is never serious, never burdened. It dances through creation in perfect harmony, delighting in all expressions of life. It is the Spirit of Lightness that forever plays in the now.

Unification: I am one with this Divine Joy. I am not separate from its laughter, its gentleness, its playfulness. The Spirit of Light lives in me, breathes through me, and invites me to let go of the weight of the world, of the illusion, and return to the lightness of Truth. I remember that I was not created for suffering, but to be an extension of divine delight.

Realization: Today, I choose to release the false belief that spiritual growth must be serious or somber. I welcome the vibration of playfulness into my day, into my heart, into my being. I allow myself to be lighthearted, to smile at the illusion, to laugh with Spirit, and to live with childlike curiosity. I embrace joy as my natural state. I give myself permission to be silly, to dance, to breathe freely, and to see the innocence in all things.

Gratitude: I am grateful for the reminder that joy is sacred. I am thankful for the Light that breaks through the cracks of heaviness. I celebrate the Divine humor that gently awakens my heart. I smile with the Infinite and let laughter become my prayer.

Release: I now release this treatment into the flow of Infinite Intelligence, knowing that all is already aligned with this uplifted Truth. I step forward in lightness, with a playful spirit and a heart full of grace.

And so it is!

Day 37: Recognizing Divine Synchronicities

"A healed mind does not plan. It carries out the plans which it receives through listening to wisdom that is not its own."
— A Course in Miracles

Recognition: There is One Divine Intelligence, vast and all-knowing, that orchestrates life with perfect timing, harmony, and purpose. This Infinite Presence moves beyond human understanding, weaving together every detail of creation into a magnificent tapestry of meaning and direction. Nothing is random in the Mind of God.

Unification: I am one with this Divine Intelligence. I am held within Its sacred pattern. My life is part of Its unfolding beauty. As I listen within, I recognize that I am not separate from Divine Order—I am an expression of it. I am guided by the same Source that governs the stars and stirs the tides.

Realization: Today, I open my awareness to the synchronicities that surround me. I notice the gentle signs, the aligned moments, the meaningful "coincidences" that are truly Spirit whispering, "I am here." I no longer dismiss these nudges—I honor them. I release the need to control and instead allow life to reveal its Divine rhythm. I trust the timing. I trust the symbols. I trust the path that is being shown, step by step, through grace.

Gratitude: I give thanks for every signpost, every aligned encounter, every perfect unfolding that reminds me I am not alone. I rejoice in the Presence that walks with me, guiding and affirming my journey. I am deeply grateful for the mystery and the magic of Divine timing.

Release: I let this truth settle deeply into my consciousness. I release this treatment into the Law of Divine Flow, where all synchronicities continue to reveal themselves as blessings.

And so it is!

Day 38: Deepening Your Surrender

"In my defenselessness my safety lies."
— *A Course in Miracles*

Recognition: There is a Presence, eternal and unchanging, that holds all things in perfect balance. This Presence is Love Itself, the Source of all wisdom, the foundation of all peace. It knows *the Way*, even when I do not. It is the Creative Force behind all that is.

Unification: I am not separate from this Infinite Presence. I am a wave within its ocean, a light within its great radiance. Divine Wisdom breathes through me, carries me, and loves me without condition. I am safely held in the arms of Grace.

Realization: I now surrender—not out of fear or helplessness, but from a deep and sacred knowing that I am supported by something far greater than my ego-based plans. I surrender the tight grip of control, the questioning, the need to figure it all out. I let go of resistance and fall into the gentle current of trust.

I allow the Holy to lead. I soften, I open, and I say yes to what is being revealed, even if I do not yet understand. I release the illusion that I must carry everything on my own.

Gratitude: Thank you, Divine Presence, for showing me that surrender is not giving up, it is returning to Truth. It is allowing You to lead. Thank you for receiving all that I lay down with love and without judgment. I am so grateful to rest in the freedom of surrender, to trust the unfolding with peace in my heart.

Release: I now release this treatment into the Law of Divine Order. It is done. The path is clear. My surrender is sacred.

And so it is!

Day 39: Walking as Love

"Teach only love, for that is what you are."
— A Course in Miracles

Recognition: There is One Infinite Presence, and Its name is Love. Pure, boundless, formless Love—unconditional, changeless, and eternal. This Love is not earned or lost. It is the fabric of the universe, the Source of all healing, and the Truth beneath all appearances.

Unification: I am not separate from this Love. I was created by Love as Love. It flows through my being, breathes through my breath, and radiates through my consciousness. Every cell, every thought, every word can become an extension of this Divine Love. I am not here to seek love—I am here to *be* Love.

Realization: Today, I choose to walk as Love. I release the need to defend, to attack, to withhold, or to protect. I see through the eyes of compassion, I listen with the ears of the heart, and I speak with the voice of gentleness and Truth. Whether I am alone or with others, I am a walking sanctuary of Love. I bless those who cross my path, those I find easy to love and those who challenge me to go deeper. Every step I take is a holy encounter, an opportunity to extend what I am. Love is not something I do—it is what walks in my place.

Gratitude: I am deeply grateful to remember my true identity as Love. I am thankful for the simplicity of this path, the softness it brings, and the strength that flows from gentleness. Thank you, Divine Presence, for guiding my heart and feet on this path of Love.

Release: I release this awareness into the Infinite Law, knowing it is already made manifest. I walk as Love, now and always.

And so it is!

Day 40: Anchoring into Your Divine Identity

"I am as God created me."
— A Course in Miracles

Recognition: There is only one Reality, one Infinite Presence, one Divine Mind from which all things arise. This Source is eternal, pure, and whole. It is unchanging Love, perfect Wisdom, radiant Light. It is the Ground of all Being—forever expressing, forever extending, forever creating in Its own likeness.

Unification: And I am One with this Divine Reality. I am not a body. I am not a name, a role, a story. I am the holy extension of Divine Mind, a spark of the Infinite Light, a wave in the great ocean of Love. I am not separate, not broken, not lost—I am found in the Truth of what I have always been. Whole. Eternal. Divine.

Realization: Today, I choose to remember who I truly am. I release all false images, all ego-identities, all illusions of unworthiness or limitation. I anchor into the stillness beneath the noise. I recognize the unshakable Truth of my being. I am Spirit—limitless, radiant, and free. Every thought aligned with Truth strengthens my awareness of my Divine Identity. I need not strive to become—I only need to remember. I walk through this world, not as its victim, but as a bringer of Light, as one who knows their Source and lives from It.

Gratitude: I am deeply grateful for this remembrance. I am thankful for the journey that has led me here—the challenges, the ego-based alarms, the awakenings, the grace. I honor the

Divine Identity in myself and in all others. We are all part of the One, waking together in Love.

Release: I now release this word, this treatment, this awareness, into the perfect activity of Divine Mind, knowing it is already so. I am anchored in my Divine Identity.

And so it is!

Conclusion: A Journey that Continues

These 40 days were never about an ending. They were a beginning, a sacred doorway back to the Truth that lives within you.

Each Spiritual Mind Treatment in this book has been an invitation to return home to your Divine Identity, to soften into Presence, and to allow Love to lead. But what you have uncovered here is not limited to these pages. It lives in your breath, your awareness, your willingness to listen deeply.

We do not stop here. We continue what we just began.

This book is yours now—a companion for your daily alignment, a prayer book to return to whenever the world feels heavy or your thoughts grow loud. Let it sit beside your journal, on your altar, or anywhere your heart calls you to reach for the sacred.

And beyond simply reading these treatments, may you begin to write your own. Your soul speaks in a language only you can translate. You now know the structure: Recognition, Unification, Realization, Gratitude, and Release. But even more important than the form is the *feeling*—the deep, inner knowing that Spirit lives in you, as you, through you. Let the voice within write them for you. Let the voice from within use a vocabulary that might not be yours, but you know is it right.

Let these prayers ripple outward. Share them in quiet moments with loved ones. Speak them into your morning. Whisper them before sleep. Offer them on behalf of someone who's hurting under the Law of Grace. Use them as blessings over your meals, your work, your travels. Let them be both anchor and wings.

You have remembered how to pray—not to ask for what you lack, but to affirm what is already whole and holy. You have remembered to pray not from a place of lack but from a place of abundance.

This is not the end of your journey. It is the opening of a new rhythm, a new way of being, and a new relationship with the Divine.

May you walk forward now, rooted in Love, guided by Truth, and radiant in your Light.

And so it is!

The following spiritual mindfulness treatments are from my journals, as well as some excerpts from my weekly episodes. I am happy to share with you a few of them that did not make the cut for this 40-day journey, but I thought you might enjoy them as much as I did.

Trusting Divine Guidance

*"If you knew Who walks beside you on the way
that you have chosen, fear would be impossible."*
— A Course in Miracles

I recognize the ever-present wisdom of the Divine, the voice of Love that whispers through every moment beyond my ego-veil, guiding me with infinite care and clarity.

I know that this Divine Guidance flows through me. It is not outside of me, but within me as a sacred compass forever tuned to the frequency of my highest good.

I trust the gentle guidance of Spirit. I release the need for control, the fear of the unknown, and the doubt that clouds my vision. I am guided with precision and love, always walking the path of my soul's unfolding purpose.

I give thanks for the Divine Intelligence that leads me. I am grateful for the signs showing me I am on my right path, the synchronicities, and the inner knowing that reassure me I am never alone.

I release this treatment into the Law of the Universe, knowing that every step I take is divinely orchestrated. I walk in trust.

And so it is!

Remembering My Wholeness

"I am as God created me."
— A Course in Miracles

I recognize the wholeness of Divine Creation, the perfect completeness that is the foundation of all existence. Nothing is missing; nothing is broken.

I know that I am a perfect expression of this Divine Wholeness. My Essence is untouched by the illusions of limitation, lack, or separation. I am whole, holy, and complete.

I remember the truth of my being. I release the belief that I need fixing, healing, or proving. I am already everything I need to be. The light of my wholeness radiates effortlessly into my life and the world.

I am profoundly grateful for the gift of wholeness. I give thanks for my soul, my mind, my body — each a sacred vessel of Divine perfection.

I release this treatment into the Infinite, knowing that my wholeness is already established. I walk in the truth of my completeness.

And so it is!

Surrendering to Divine Flow

> *"I need do nothing."*
> — A Course in Miracles

I recognize the perfect flow of Divine Intelligence, the effortless unfolding of life as an expression of Infinite Wisdom and Love.

I know that I am part of this Divine Flow. I am not separate from the natural rhythm of the Universe. Life moves through me and as me.

I surrender the need to force, push, or control. I trust the current of Divine Will to carry me exactly where I am meant to be. I release resistance and allow life to unfold with grace and ease.

I am deeply grateful for the peace that comes with surrender. I give thanks for the knowing that everything is already perfectly aligned for my highest good.

I release this treatment into the Law of the Universe, knowing that all is well, and I am held in the Divine Flow.

And so it is!

Embracing Inner Peace

"Nothing real can be threatened. Nothing unreal exists. Herein lies the peace of God."
— A Course in Miracles

I recognize the Infinite Presence of Peace, the stillness that surpasses all understanding, ever-present and unwavering in the heart of creation.

I align myself with this Divine Peace, knowing it is my birthright and my natural state of being. I feel this peace expanding within me, dissolving tension, quieting the restless mind, and enveloping me in a gentle serenity.

I release all chaotic thoughts, all disturbances, and all fearful projections of the ego-based past or future. I surrender the need to fix or control, trusting that peace is not something to be attained, but something to be remembered within me.

I declare that peace flows through my being like a tranquil stream, washing over every aspect of my life. I see peace in my relationships, my body, my work, and my path.

I am grateful for this abiding calm, for the knowing that I am always held in the embrace of Divine Peace.

I release this word into the Divine Law of creation, trusting that this peace is already established, now and forever.

And so it is!

Awaken to Divine Love

> *"Love holds no grievances."*
> — *A Course in Miracles*

I recognize Love as the very Essence of the Divine, the unchanging force that breathes life into all things.

I align my heart with this Infinite Love, feeling its warmth dissolve any sense of separation or judgment. Love flows through me, touching every cell of my being, awakening my soul to its true nature.

I release all grievances, all barriers to love, and all stories of unworthiness. I let go of the belief that love must be earned, recognizing that I am Love, whole and complete.

I declare that Love radiates from me, effortlessly blessing every interaction, every thought, and every corner of my life. Love heals, restores, and uplifts everything it touches.

I am grateful for this boundless Love, for the miracle of seeing the world through eyes of compassion and grace.

I release this word into Divine Law, knowing Love is my eternal Truth, now and forever.

And so it is!

Discovering Inner Strength

"I am sustained by the love of God."
— A Course in Miracles

I recognize the Infinite Power of Spirit, an unshakable strength that is the foundation of all life.

I align myself with this divine strength, feeling it rise within me like a steady flame. I know that this strength is not of the ego, but of the soul — a power that cannot be diminished or lost.

I release all beliefs in limitation, weakness, or struggle. I let go of the idea that I must carry life alone, remembering that divine strength flows through me with every breath.

I declare that I am resilient, courageous, and divinely equipped to meet every experience with grace. I trust in my ability to stand tall, not through force, but through my connection to the Infinite.

I am grateful for this inner fortitude, for the quiet power that sustains me through all seasons of life.

I release this word into Divine Law, knowing that I am already strengthened, already supported, already whole.

And so it is!

About the Author

Dr. Nathalie Turgeon, Ph.D., is a spiritual teacher, metaphysical practitioner, and conscious guide whose life is a living testament to the wisdom she shares. With a few decades of direct experience as a counselor, her true initiation began long before credentials or titles—rooted in a deep inner calling that shaped her path from an early age.

Her journey has not followed a straight line, but one of sacred detours, necessary forgetting, and purposeful returns to *the Way*. Like many seekers, she wandered more than once far from the Truth she now teaches—not out of failure, but to embody understanding, compassion, and mastery from within. Each step away brought her closer to the realization that she was never truly lost, only gathering what she needed to one day guide others home to themselves, without judgment.

What sets Dr. Nathalie apart is that she teaches only what she has lived. She has always wanted to "walk the talk." Her insights are not borrowed theories but hard-earned revelations—collected through her own ego-surrendering experiences, moments of grace, visions, and deep inner work. Her mission is clear: to help others free their mind, free themselves from ego illusion, awaken to their Higher Self, and live from pure Love.

In her 50s, she went back to school, following an inner call to expand her studies. She holds a Ph.D. in Philosophy with a specialization in Metaphysical Counseling. She made it her mission to explore, for her dissertation, the topic of gratitude: *Gratitude as a Spiritual Mind Treatment for Mental Health*, following her master's thesis on *Reaching the Summit of Consciousness Through Meditation Like Great Masters and Prophets Did*.

While she self-published workbooks on gratitude, Ho'oponopono, and faith, it is only recently that she stepped fully into her lifelong dream of allowing her inner author to share knowingness in book format—speaking not just to the mind, but awakening something beyond the ego veils, allowing the soul to shine through. Whether writing, teaching, or simply being, Dr. Nathalie transmits spiritual truth as one who *is* it.

Her core message and her mantra?
"Breathe In, let go of all your ego-based thoughts and vision, see from your Soul… and Love Out."

nathalieturgeon.com

breatheinloveoutcenter.com

www.ingramcontent.com/pod-product-compliance
Lightning Source LLC
Chambersburg PA
CBHW051606010526
44119CB00056B/799